JODY O'NEILL

Jody O'Neill is a writer and actor. She graduated with a Bachelor in Acting Studies from Trinity College in 2003.

She is part of Rough Magic's ADVANCE programme and has spent the past two years researching, developing and making work that promotes Autism acceptance.

Working with Draíocht and Blakestown Adult Day Centre, Jody recently developed a new work, *Saying the Words,* that was performed on Culture Night 2019 as part of Draíocht's 'Our Place Our Stories'. She has a keen interest in creating relaxed performances in inclusive settings.

In 2019, Jody was awarded a Judges' Commendation in the Bruntwood Prize for Playwriting (Europe's biggest playwriting prize), she was shortlisted for the PJ O'Connor Award, and was one of the six final playwrights shortlisted for Fishamble's A Play for Ireland. Her play *Eating the City* was selected to be part of The New Theatre's 2019 *Path to the Stage* New Writing Week.

Recent work includes *Scrapefoot* (Anu Productions/The Ark) and *Yellow* (HOME Theatre Ireland/Draíocht).

Other writing work includes *The Juniper Tree* for the Abbey Theatre, *It's a Lovely Day, Bill Withers* (Fishamble's Tiny Plays for Ireland), *Walking Man* (Graffiti Theatre Company), *Celebrity,* produced by Peer to Peer (shortlisted for the 2011 Stewart Parker Trust Awards) and *They Never Froze Walt Disney,* produced by Theatre Makers (nominated for Dublin Fringe Festival New Writing Award 2008).

From 2014–2018, Jody was a regular script and story writer for RTÉ's *Fair City.*

Other Titles in this Series

Annie Baker
THE ANTIPODES
THE FLICK
JOHN

Mike Bartlett
ALBION
BULL
GAME
AN INTERVENTION
KING CHARLES III
SNOWFLAKE
VASSA *after* Gorky
WILD

Chris Bush
THE ASSASSINATION OF
    KATIE HOPKINS
THE CHANGING ROOM
FAUSTUS: THAT DAMNED WOMAN
THE LAST NOËL
STEEL

Jez Butterworth
THE FERRYMAN
JERUSALEM
JEZ BUTTERWORTH PLAYS: ONE
MOJO
THE NIGHT HERON
PARLOUR SONG
THE RIVER
THE WINTERLING

Caryl Churchill
BLUE HEART
CHURCHILL PLAYS: THREE
CHURCHILL PLAYS: FOUR
CHURCHILL PLAYS: FIVE
CHURCHILL: SHORTS
CLOUD NINE
DING DONG THE WICKED
A DREAM PLAY *after* Strindberg
DRUNK ENOUGH TO SAY I LOVE YOU?
ESCAPED ALONE
FAR AWAY
GLASS. KILL. BLUEBEARD'S FRIENDS.
    IMP.
HERE WE GO
HOTEL
ICECREAM
LIGHT SHINING IN BUCKINGHAMSHIRE
LOVE AND INFORMATION
MAD FOREST
A NUMBER
PIGS AND DOGS
SEVEN JEWISH CHILDREN
THE SKRIKER
THIS IS A CHAIR
THYESTES *after* Seneca
TRAPS

debbie tucker green
BORN BAD
DEBBIE TUCKER GREEN PLAYS: ONE
DIRTY BUTTERFLY
EAR FOR EYE
HANG
NUT
A PROFOUNDLY AFFECTIONATE,
    PASSIONATE DEVOTION TO
    SOMEONE (– *NOUN*)
RANDOM
STONING MARY
TRADE & GENERATIONS
TRUTH AND RECONCILIATION

Stacey Gregg
LAGAN
OVERRIDE
PERVE
SCORCH
SHIBBOLETH
WHEN COWS GO BOOM

Nancy Harris
THE BEACON
NO ROMANCE
OUR NEW GIRL
THE RED SHOES
TWO LADIES

Deirdre Kinahan
CROSSINGS
HALCYON DAYS
MOMENT
RATHMINES ROAD
SPINNING
THE UNMANAGEABLE SISTERS
    after Michel Tremblay

Lucy Kirkwood
BEAUTY AND THE BEAST
    with Katie Mitchell
BLOODY WIMMIN
THE CHILDREN
CHIMERICA
HEDDA *after* Ibsen
IT FELT EMPTY WHEN THE HEART
    WENT AT FIRST BUT IT IS
    ALRIGHT NOW
LUCY KIRKWOOD PLAYS: ONE
MOSQUITOES
NSFW
TINDERBOX
THE WELKIN

Chinonyerem Odimba
AMONGST THE REEDS
PRINCESS & THE HUSTLER
UNKNWN RIVERS

Bijan Sheibani
THE ARRIVAL

Stef Smith
ENOUGH
GIRL IN THE MACHINE
HUMAN ANIMALS
NORA : A DOLL'S HOUSE *after* Ibsen
REMOTE
SWALLOW

Jack Thorne
2ND MAY 1997
BUNNY
BURYING YOUR BROTHER IN
    THE PAVEMENT
A CHRISTMAS CAROL *after* Dickens
THE END OF HISTORY…
HOPE
JACK THORNE PLAYS: ONE
JUNKYARD
LET THE RIGHT ONE IN
    after John Ajvide Lindqvist
MYDIDAE
THE SOLID LIFE OF SUGAR WATER
STACY & FANNY AND FAGGOT
WHEN YOU CURE ME
WOYZECK *after* Büchner

Phoebe Waller-Bridge
FLEABAG

Jody O'Neill

WHAT I (DON'T) KNOW ABOUT KNOW ABOUT AUTISM

NICK HERN BOOKS
London
www.nickhernbooks.co.uk

A Nick Hern Book

What I (Don't) Know About Autism first published in Great Britain in 2020 as a paperback original by Nick Hern Books Limited, The Glasshouse, 49a Goldhawk Road, London W12 8QP

What I (Don't) Know About Autism copyright © 2020 Jody O'Neill

Jody O'Neill has asserted her moral right to be identified as the author of this work

Designed and typeset by Nick Hern Books, London
Printed in Great Britain by Mimeo Ltd, Huntingdon, Cambridgeshire PE29 6XX

A CIP catalogue record for this book is available from the British Library

ISBN   978 1 84842 949 9

What I (Don't) Know About Autism opened at the Abbey
Theatre, Dublin, on the Peacock Stage, on 4 February 2020
(previews from 1 February) and was also performed at The
Everyman, Cork, and Mermaid County Wicklow Arts Centre.
The cast was as follows:

Shay Croke
Paula McGlinchey
Jayson Murray
Jody O'Neill
Matthew Ralli
Eleanor Walsh

Director	Dónal Gallagher
Choreographer	Cindy Cummings
Set and Costume Designer	Medb Lambert
Lighting Designer	Eoin Winning
Composer and Sound Designer	Carl Kennedy
Production Manager	Anthony Hanley
Stage Manager	Cian Mulhall
Assistant Stage Manager	Shannon Cowan
Press	Dairne O'Sullivan
Marketing	Fergus Hannigan
Graphic Design	BLAM / ZOO.
Producer	Melissa Nolan
Autism Consultant	Eleanor Walsh

**ABBEY
THEATRE
AMHARCLANN
NA MAINISTREACH**

Abbey Theatre | Amharclann na Mainistreach

The Abbey Theatre is Ireland's National Theatre. It was founded by W.B. Yeats and Lady Augusta Gregory. Since it first opened its doors in 1904 the theatre has played a vital role in the artistic, social and cultural life of Ireland.

Inspired by the revolutionary ideals of its founders and its rich canon of Irish dramatic writing, the Abbey Theatre's mission is to imaginatively engage with all of Irish society through the production of ambitious, courageous and new theatre in all its forms. The Abbey Theatre commits to lead in the telling of the whole Irish story, in English and in Irish, and affirms that it is a theatre for the entire island of Ireland and for all its people. In every endeavour, the Abbey Theatre promotes inclusiveness, diversity and equality.

The Abbey Theatre gratefully acknowledges the support of the Arts Council.

Acknowledgements

Funded by the Arts Council, Wicklow County Council and Dublin City Council with the support of The Everyman, the Abbey Theatre, Mermaid Arts Centre, AsIAm, Fishamble New Play Clinic, Rough Magic Theatre Company, KCAT and Triple A Wicklow.

8

Characters

ONE
TWO
THREE
FOUR
FIVE
SIX

Who play

VOICE
INTERRUPTING VOICE
KID
TEACHER
PARENT
PIANO TEACHER
JONATHAN
PHOTOGRAPHER
A MOTHER
FATHER
SON
COLM
HIM, *Colm's thoughts*
SANDRA
HER, *Sandra's thoughts*
SANDRA'S MUM
DOCTOR
ASSISTANT
TERENCE
GINA
BEATRICE
SIMON
PARENT ONE
PARENT TWO
MOTHER

INTERVIEWER
CASPER
PARENT
CHILD
PHS, *Public Health Service*
WOMAN – PHS
WOMAN – LATER LIFE
GORDON
GORDON'S MUM
GORDON'S DAD

And WAITERS, *a* CHILD, SECURITY GUARDS

Note on Text

The play is written to be performed by a cast of both autistic and non-autistic actors.

It's important that INTERRUPTING VOICE and VOICE are played by the same actors throughout.

For ease of rehearsals, where actors were not playing an assigned characters, the numbers ONE to SIX were assigned.

This text went to press before the end of rehearsals and so may differ slightly from the play as performed.

A theatre space. There are flipcharts on either side of the stage with the titles of the scenes written on them.

ONE. Hello everyone and welcome to this performance of *What I (Don't) Know About Autism*. Before we begin, there are a few things we wanted to say.

TWO. This play is a relaxed performance. If you need to leave the theatre during the performance, that's okay. And if you'd like to come back in again, that's fine too.

THREE. If you need to make noise or move around during the performance, we're grand with that.

FOUR. If the person beside you is making noise or moving during the performance, please don't feel like you need to shush them.

FIVE. Everything is okay. The house lights will remain on during the show. So, even though the stage might go dark, there will always be light where you are sitting.

SIX. If you have a mobile phone, please don't leave the volume on or use the phone during the performance unless you have to.

FOUR. The play is fifty-eight pages long. That means it will last about eighty minutes. It's broken into twenty-six scenes, and you can see the names of the scenes on the flipcharts here.

SIX. When a scene is finished, we'll cross it out.

TWO. That way, you can keep track of how long has passed, and how long is left.

FIVE. As you can see, the play is also captioned. That means that everything we say will appear back there.

FIVE *gestures to the scrim.*

ONE. There are some loud noises during the performance. If you are sensitive to loud noises, please feel free to wear your ear defenders or ear plugs during that part. We'll let you know in advance if there's a loud bit coming up, so that you have time to put them on.

THREE. The front-of-house staff have some spare sets of ear defenders if anyone needs them. Does anyone need ear defenders? If you do, just put your hand up now.

If anyone requires ear defenders, front-of-house staff or actors can deliver them.

Or if you decide during the show that you need ear defenders, you can come and get them from this box.

SIX. There will be a twenty-minute talkback after the show. You can stay for this if you like, but if you'd prefer not to, that's fine too.

FIVE. In the extremely unlikely event of an emergency, the fire exits are here and here.

FOUR. That's it. We hope you enjoy the show.

1. The Beginning

TWO (*to* ONE). This is a relaxed performance.

Relax.

You don't look relaxed.

Look at me.

You're not looking in my eye.

How are you ever going to get a job if you can't look someone in the eye?

THREE. According to the National Autistic Society in the UK, only sixteen per cent of autistic adults are in full-time employment. Many employers agree lack of eye contact is a strong reason not to hire someone.

TWO. It's a sign you're not trustworthy.

THREE. It's a sign you're dishonest.

TWO. It's a sign you've got something to hide.

ONE. I'll tell you what I'm hiding. Looking at you hurts me. Looking at you confuses me. Looking at you is like coming face-to-face with a black hole. Whatever is in my head, the second I look in your eyes, and try to tell you, or try to listen. It's sucked away. It's gone in an instant.

FOUR. My name is Megan. I have a diagnosis of high-functioning autism, with an ounce of OCD and a lorry-load of dyspraxia. I am autistic. I am unemployed.

SIX. My name is Peter. I have a diagnosis of Asperger's, with acute anxiety, and a peanut allergy. I am autistic. I am unemployed.

THREE (*shaking hands with audience members*). My name is Alison. My name is Alison. My name is Alison. My name is

Alison. I have moderate to severe autism, depending on who you choose to believe. I also had an intellectual disability diagnosis, but dropped that after I published my first book. I am autistic.

TWO. My name is Mary. I have six ounces of anxiety, a scar on my left knee, a teensy bit of racial bias and a fear of walking alone at night. I am neurotypical.

INTERRUPTING VOICE. Neuro-what?

SIX. Neurotypical. It basically means non-autistic.

FOUR. It started out as a joke, but actually led to the whole neurodiversity movement. (*Maybe a look from* SIX – *'time is ticking'*.) We'll come back to that later.

INTERRUPTING VOICE. Thanks.

SIX. No problem. (*To the audience*.) It's okay to ask questions.

INTERRUPTING VOICE. Is it?

SIX. Sorry?

INTERRUPTING VOICE. Is it actually okay to ask questions? It's just… it really bugs me when people say things like – (*Mimicking*.) 'It's okay to ask questions', if it's not really okay.

SIX. It is okay.

INTERRUPTING VOICE. When?

SIX. What?

INTERRUPTING VOICE. When is it okay? Can anybody ask a question at any time? Because that could get tricky.

FOUR. Okay, fine. We'll have designated question times during the show. (*To the control room*.) Could I get a light here, please? Whenever this light comes on – (*A light comes on*.) we will all go to the designated question area and they can ask questions. (*To the audience*.) Okay?

INTERRUPTING VOICE. For how long? Because we still have fifty-five pages to get through. And we don't want the show to become an indefinitely long Q&A session. So, how long?

ONE *steps forward, proffering a tiny egg timer.*

ONE. You can use this if you like.

FOUR. Thanks. Eh – it's a bit small.

ONE *takes back the small timer. Returns with giant timer.*

Better. But it only times sixty seconds.

SIX *is getting impatient.*

Two turns of the timer. Okay?

INTERRUPTING VOICE. Okay. And if nobody asks
a question?

SIX. We just carry on with the show.

ONE. My name is Michael. I like my bread with only the tiniest
scraping of butter. I struggle with the concept of sauce.
I don't like the smell of other people's breath in the morning,
but I can't stand to sleep alone. I am neurotypical.

FIVE. My name is James. I don't like labels. One of my
siblings has 'high-functioning autism', but on a bad day, she
can hardly dress herself. My other sibling has 'severe
autism'. People write him off as soon as he enters the room,
but they'd reconsider if they saw his artwork. Apparently,
I'm neurotypical.

ALL. My name is Casper. I am not here.

2. Isolation

FOUR. I know these two things are true: One – We are all more alike than we are different. Two – If you've met one person with autism, you've met one person with autism.

FIVE. I don't know what's real and what's not real.

TWO. I don't know who my friends are.

SIX. I don't know what to think.

ONE. I don't know why I can't feel happiness.

SIX. I don't know why photos of other people's kids grate on me so much.

FIVE. I don't know why black holes are letting stuff out when they were supposed to keep it locked up inside.

THREE. I don't know why I hurt myself, but I do.

An isolation room.

KID. The first time I found myself in here, I was five.
They told me autistic people like to be in confined places.
I didn't know what 'autistic' was.

I just wanted to get out.

A parent–teacher meeting.

TEACHER. He hit me.

PARENT. Why?

TEACHER. What do you mean, why?

PARENT. Sam doesn't hit for no reason. What did you do?

TEACHER. He was being uncooperative.

PARENT. In what way?

TEACHER. He wouldn't look at me when I was talking to him. I asked him a question and he refused to respond. He wasn't staying on the task. I offered stickers, but he refuses to be motivated by rewards.

PARENT. Was he interested in the task?

TEACHER. Sorry?

PARENT. Sam's not a dog. Did it occur to you to give him a task he was actually interested in? Did it occur to you that he might be bored?

TEACHER. I have thirty students to attend to, I can't be expected to pander to the whims of one.

PARENT. Corey has a nut allergy. Do you accommodate that?

TEACHER. Obviously. But that's a life-and-death situation.

PARENT. So, you don't consider well-being a priority?

TEACHER. That's not what I'm saying.

PARENT. When children hurt themselves, you look after them, surely?

TEACHER. Obviously.

PARENT. So, why not attend to the needs of my child?

TEACHER. Because they don't make any sense.

PARENT. To you.

TEACHER. To any sane person.

PARENT. And now you're implying my child is insane?

TEACHER *leaves*. PARENT *addresses audience*.

When I arrive at the school, I discover Sam has been kept in isolation for three hours. 'For his own good.' His knuckles are bleeding from where he has attempted to punch his way out. His nails are broken and ragged where he tried to pull the lock away from the door. His head is bruised from banging and banging it with the frustration of realising nobody was coming to let him out, and that there was nothing he could do about it. He is in a state of panic, can't catch his breath, can't get the words out, no voice. All this because he wanted to stay inside and draw during the lunch break instead of going out to the yard. They call it non-compliance. When I make a formal complaint to the board of management, I get back a solicitor's letter and an invoice for damage to the isolation room.

THREE. Definition: Isolation, seclusion or withdrawal rooms are spaces in schools where so-called 'disruptive' children can be sent to take time out.

ONE. Along with physical restraint, their use in Irish classrooms is unregulated by the Department of Education, and at the discretion of the teacher in charge.

KID. They left me there to rot.

3. ABA

A piano teacher prepares to give a teenager, JONATHAN, *a piano lesson.*

TEACHER. Jonathan.

JONATHAN *sits down.*

A.

She plays the note and JONATHAN *copies, playing the note.*

JONATHAN. A.

TEACHER. Good playing.

TEACHER *plays another note.*

C.

JONATHAN *copies, playing the note.*

JONATHAN. C.

TEACHER. Very good 'C'.

Plays another note.

G.

JONATHAN *copies, playing the note.*

JONATHAN. G.

TEACHER. Good 'G'. Well done. Now try, A.

    JONATHAN *copies, playing the note*.

JONATHAN. A.

TEACHER. AB.

    JONATHAN *copies, playing the notes*.

JONATHAN. AB.

TEACHER. Good playing 'AB'. Now… ABC.

    JONATHAN *copies, playing the notes*.

JONATHAN. ABC.

TEACHER. Now, ABA.

    JONATHAN *spins a fidget spinner*.

    ABA.

    JONATHAN *spins*.

    Come on, ABA.

    JONATHAN *spins*.

    ABA, A–B–A, ABA. Come on. ABA, ABA, ABA.

    JONATHAN *spins*. TEACHER *grabs the spinner.*

    You can have this back when you play the right notes.

    JONATHAN *hits random keys creating total dissonance*. TEACHER *speaks over the noise*.

    ABA or Applied Behavioural Analysis was developed by B.F. Skinner and Ivar Lovaas.

    ONE *interrupts*.

ONE. Yes, that's the same Ivar Lovaas that pioneered gay conversion therapy.

TEACHER. It comes from the training of dogs or animals. It is based around the idea of performing a task for a reward.

Motivation. You can probably think of examples where you use ABA in your own everyday life. You go for a run, you get a cup of coffee, maybe even a brownie if you've done especially well. You put in a hard week's work, Friday evening, you get a bottle of wine and order takeaway.

JONATHAN. For me, ABA was like this:

I like flapping my hands.

TEACHER. Quiet hands.

JONATHAN. I like sucking my fingers and my thumbs.

TEACHER. Hands down.

JONATHAN. I like to hum. It keeps me calm. It's a layer of protection between me and the world.

TEACHER. Quiet.

JONATHAN. Am I hurting you? Am I doing something wrong?

JONATHAN *looks at* TEACHER. TEACHER *looks at* JONATHAN.

4. Our Problem Child

A MOTHER, FATHER *and* SON *pose for a family portrait. A* PHOTOGRAPHER *directs them.*

PHOTOGRAPHER. And three, two, one… (*Takes photo.*) Lovely.

A MOTHER. He's always been difficult. Always our problem child, weren't you? I put it down to him being an only child for a long time, but then when he didn't start talking, we realised there was something else going on.

PHOTOGRAPHER. Can you look up here for me, Harry?

Okay. That'll do. Everyone say, 'Cheese.'

Photo.

A MOTHER. Look at him there. He's not even listening. You could say anything and it would make no difference to him.

PHOTOGRAPHER. Could you give us a smile, Harry?

SON *responds.*

That's it.

MOTHER *grabs his face to make him smile.*

Okay. Okay. And...

Photo.

A MOTHER. Don't you think it would drive a person crazy to be looking at that, day in day out? I mean, he's like a shell.

HER SON. I remember everything. I remember it all. All my life you've talked about me like I'm not here. So, I left.

Or I tried to.

I took as much of myself away as I possibly could.

My mind flies up the chimney, but your voice calls me back.

A MOTHER. And those sounds that come out of him. Like an animal. In seventeen years, he's never said a coherent word. And he doesn't feel anything.

She hits him. He doesn't react.

See? Nothing. He's like a machine. Hyposensitivity, they call it.

HER SON. I just grew a thick skin. I stopped reacting once I knew it would only make things worse.

PHOTOGRAPHER. How about we swap places? Dad, you can come down here. That's it. And heads to the camera. Three, two, one...

Photo.

A MOTHER. I mean, of course, I love him. He's my son but he has no way of loving me back.

PHOTOGRAPHER. Let's get one with just the guys, father and son. Mum, you're doing great. Take a little rest.

PHOTOGRAPHER *is about to take a photo when they are interrupted.*

A MOTHER. Can you imagine what that's like? To never have your child tell you that they love you back.

HER SON. I tried to tell you, but you wouldn't listen. It had to be your way or not at all.

In my mind, I hear the words, but I can't trap the sounds, hold them long enough in my mouth to shape them and send them to you.

The scene freezes. They turn to face the audience.

ALL FOUR. My name is Casper. I am not here.

5. Stimming

THREE. There will be loud noises.

A low-key choreographed stimming sequence develops during the following.

FOUR. Definition: Self-stimulatory behaviour, also known as stimming, is the repetition of movements, sounds, or words, or the repetitive manipulation of objects, common in people with autism.

It's not that other people don't stim, but autistic people do it in style.

For a neurotypical person, stimming might consist of pacing while on the phone, tapping their fingers on the table, chewing their pen. For someone with autism, their stims might be bigger – hand-flapping, spinning, vocal tics, rocking.

ALL. Quiet hands!

They stop their stims.

THREE. I love stimming. It regulates me, makes me feel happy, helps me to stay in control. The downside is that sometimes the places you most need to stim, are the places where stimming would be least accepted. I have a vision of a world where you can stim wherever you want. Or at least, with designated stimming zones. Smokers in that corner, stimmers letting loose over here. But my dream is a bit of a way off from becoming a reality.

In the meantime, what am I supposed to do? Hold it in until I get home?

6. Question Time

SIX (*to the audience*). Does anyone have any questions about what we have done so far in the play?

The timer is turned. The audience may or may not ask questions.

7. First Date

The lights are low. A romantic date. Music begins to play.
All the sounds are amplified and grow louder as the scene
progresses. His fork on the plate. His and her eating sounds.
Waiters dropping cutlery in the background. Tables too close
together. People whizzing by. General chitchat. Too-loud music.
We hear COLM *and* SANDRA*'s thoughts.*

HIM. She looks happy enough.

HER. I hope I don't seem too jumpy. Jesus! Why do they keep
    dropping everything?

HIM. I wonder if she'd like my dog story? Does she even like
    dogs?

HER. Am I looking at him enough?

HIM. Some girls like cats better.

HER. Am I looking at him too much?

HIM. She could be allergic.

HER. Who ever thought restaurants were good places for a first
    date, anyway?

HIM. Maybe it's not that funny, anyway.

HER. Is it an endurance test? I wish I'd suggested going to the
    zoo. At least we could have talked about the animals.

HIM. She has a really attractive mouth. I don't think I've ever
    seen someone chew with so much grace.

    She drops her fork.

HER. He's going to think I'm such a klutz. What would he
    say if I told him I only figured out how to use a knife three
    years ago?

    A WAITER *rushes over to replace her fork. She jumps.*

    Why do they have to do that? I could have wiped it.

HIM. It's funny how they do that. Like, the fork's been on the
    ground for seconds. She could wipe it. Plus, aren't we

blatantly ignoring the salient fact that this fork has previously spent time in hundreds of people's mouths?

HER. There's a stain on this fork. Now, I can't stop thinking about whose mouth it was in last. Oh shit. I wonder if he'd mind if I used my spoon?

He notices she is a little distracted. Begins to talk to her.

COLM. Is your food okay?

SANDRA. It's really good, yeah.

She pushes the plate away.

Just stuffed, you know.

HER. I'm starving.

COLM. Do you mind if I taste it?

HIM. Does she know how much this cost? There's no way I'm leaving any food behind.

HER. This is painful. Now I have to watch him eat.

An awkward pause.

COLM. I'd a feeling you'd like this place.

SANDRA. Oh?

COLM. Yeah. Do you?

SANDRA. Honestly? It's like having dinner in a train station.

COLM (*amused*). Yeah?

SANDRA. You know. The noise, everyone zooming around.

COLM. I guess. Never thought of it like a train station before. Unique selling point.

SANDRA *is reaching her threshold with the noise and stimulation.*

SANDRA. Sorry?

COLM. Do you want dessert?

SANDRA. No. I'm... I actually have to meet someone.

COLM. Oh.

SANDRA. Sorry.

COLM. No, that's cool. I'll get the bill.

He goes to pay the bill and we go inside SANDRA*'s head where she and* COLM *perform a duet, complete with backing dancers. Words arranged to the tune of Journey's 'Don't Stop Believing'.*

ONE (*to audience*). Loud music, singing and dancing coming up.

COLM. She's an autistic girl
    Livin' in a neurotypical world
    She takes a trip on Tinder
    To see where it goes.

SANDRA. I fill my profile in
    Filling it with anything
    Anything except the fact
    My life runs along a different track.

COLM. She waits a day or two
    Nothing but dick pics coming through
    About to take it down
    When she meets you.

BOTH. Online, it's easy
    to express those feelings.
    Back and forth joking
    All night long.

COLM. Dinner-date looming
    It's moving on too quickly
    Sitting at the table
    Nowhere to run…

BOTH. Don't stim this evening.
    Hold in that feeling.
    Don't stim this evening.
    He won't understand

    Don't let yourself down
    You've worked so hard

Small taps and hand flaps
While he pays the bill
Turn down his invite
To have a drink around the corner
Loud noise, and bad smells, time to go...

SANDRA *leaves. A stimming sequence becomes a dance.*
It is wild, ebullient and expresses utter freedom.

The fantasy ends and COLM *returns from paying the bill to*
find that SANDRA *is gone.*

8. Myths About Autism

ONE. We have no feelings.

THREE. We can't experience empathy.

TWO. We are locked in.

SIX. If you could only take the autism away, you'd be left with a normal person.

FOUR. If you can teach us to be normal, we will have a better chance of success.

FIVE. Autism means having no imagination.

ONE. Autism means we are incapable of love.

THREE. Sometimes, we don't react. That makes it okay to talk about us in front of us.

TWO. Autism is a deficit.

SIX. Autism steals children away from their parents.

FOUR. Autism needs to be treated.

FIVE. Autism needs to be cured.

ONE. Autism is a tragedy.

THREE. Autism is caused by vaccines.

FOUR. Autism can be treated with a bleach solution.

INTERRUPTING VOICE. I'm sorry, what?

VOICE. What?

INTERRUPTING VOICE. Did you just say autism can be treated with a 'beach solution'?

VOICE. I said, 'bleach'.

INTERRUPTING VOICE. Oh, okay.

VOICE. How is it okay?

INTERRUPTING VOICE. Well, whatever works, I guess.

VOICE. It doesn't work.

INTERRUPTING VOICE. What do they do with it?

VOICE. They call it Miracle Mineral Solution (MMS). It's industrial bleach. They mix it with fruit juice and feed it to their kiddos.

INTERRUPTING VOICE. And what does it do?

VOICE. Well, at worst it kills them. Other possibilities include: nausea, vomiting, diarrhoea, shedding of internal mucous membranes, kidney failure. But hey, if it yields results.

INTERRUPTING VOICE. And does it?

VOICE. No.

INTERRUPTING VOICE. No?

VOICE. There's absolutely no evidence that it does.

INTERRUPTING VOICE. Seriously, though. Nobody here would buy into that crap.

VOICE. You think? In 2018, a Kildare man lost his appeal against a conviction for manufacturing that stuff to sell to the Irish market. And believe me, the market is there.

INTERRUPTING VOICE. Come on –

VOICE. In late 2017, it was reported that a HSE worker had been accused of buying it from Poland and feeding it to her non-verbal –

ONE. I prefer the term 'non-speaking'.

VOICE. Okay – of feeding it to her non-speaking autistic child.

INTERRUPTING VOICE. Christ.

VOICE. A Health Service Executive employee. Nice, huh?

INTERRUPTING VOICE. But you'll always get some weirdos.

VOICE. In 2016, a Belfast doctor was struck off the UK's General Medical Council for recommending MMS to parents.

INTERRUPTING VOICE. Shit.

VOICE. And in 2017, the media reported that a Dublin banker had been accused of feeding his son bleach for over two years. This, despite the fact that the kid was 'continuously vomiting', 'looking very weak and losing weight'.

INTERRUPTING VOICE. Wow.

VOICE. Yeah.

ALL. My name is Casper. I am not here.

9. I've Met Someone

SANDRA *and her* MUM *are having lunch in a café.* SANDRA *is doing all she can not to be grossed out by her mother's eating noises.*

SANDRA. How's Dad?

MUM. He's grand. You know your dad.

SANDRA. How's Gran?

MUM. Good. Her hip's much better.

    Silence.

SANDRA. I've met someone.

MUM. That's nice. (*It isn't.*) Where did you meet?

SANDRA. Tinder.

MUM *doesn't approve*.

What?

MUM. Nothing.

SANDRA. No, come on. You might as well spit it out.

MUM. It's just… Tinder.

SANDRA. Lots of people meet that way.

MUM. But they're not like you, are they?

SANDRA. Meaning?

MUM. I just… there are people out there that would take advantage of people like you.

SANDRA. I can keep myself safe.

MUM. Can you?

SANDRA. For starters, I have a strict policy not to respond to anyone who sends me a willy photo.

MUM. Do people do that?

SANDRA *shows her mother her phone*. MUM *is half-fascinated, half-disgusted. She gets too interested*. SANDRA *grabs her phone back*.

SANDRA. Mum!

MUM. Okay, well that's a good rule to begin with. But what about other people?

SANDRA. I'm pretty discerning. It doesn't take me long to work out whether I like them or not.

MUM. I'm just worried you might miss some of the more subtle signals.

SANDRA. Wasn't that what all the social skills classes were for?

A stalemate.

MUM. I don't know.

SANDRA. He's nice.

MUM. You've met him?

SANDRA. We had dinner.

MUM. Oh!

SANDRA. In a restaurant.

MUM. Right. And did you tell him?

SANDRA. Not yet.

MUM. Are you planning to?

SANDRA. Maybe. That's if he even agrees to meet me again. I left pretty abruptly.

MUM. I think you should be up front. If you think it's going to be serious. He might have expectations.

SANDRA. *I* have expectations.

MUM. I know you do. But he might have different expectations. What if he wants children?

SANDRA. What if *I* want children?

MUM (*surprised*). What?

SANDRA. I've weighed it up. One: Overall worldwide population trends; Two: Environmental factors; Three: How sleep deprivation might impact overall functioning; Four: Work versus satisfaction.

MUM. What's the verdict?

SANDRA. I'd like one child, preferably female, vegetarian, about as autistic as I am. But not for five years.

MUM *absorbs this information, careful not to reveal too much.*

You don't approve.

MUM. It's not that.

SANDRA. Come on. You've got that face.

MUM. What face?

SANDRA. The 'how am I going to argue this without sending her into a meltdown?' face.

MUM. Oh?

SANDRA. Yes.

MUM. You know, for someone who's meant to struggle with reading facial expressions, you're awfully perceptive.

SANDRA. Thank you.

I've met this guy once. I'm not having babies just yet.

MUM. Just be careful, okay?

10. A Brief History of Autism in Song

THREE. Loud noise, singing and dancing coming up.

This is the history of autism.
It's been around since
We don't know when
Don't know when
Don't know whe-en

Looking back, we like to say.
Who was autistic in their day.
But given the lack of diagnostic procedure,
Retro-diagnosis is purely conjecture;

But we're going to do it anyway.

Famous people
possibly autistic
possibly autistic
possibly autistic

Youbedobe do do,
hi,
youbedo
doooooo

Sir Isaac Newton, Albert Einstein.
Nicola Tesla, ahead of his time.

Michelangelo, Emily Dickinson.
Hans Christian Andersen and Charles Darwin.
The biologist behind evol-oo-oo-oo-tion.

We're guessing by their characteristics
but way back then there were no statistics

Youbedobe do do,
hi,
youbedo
doooooo

So,
Let's fast-forward to the 1940s.
A grim time for those with disabilities.
Lock them up in an institution,
Or even worse – the eugenics solution.

Autism was known
as childhood schizophrenia
A condition you'd outgrow,
or that'd be the end of ya.

Enter stage right, Dr Leo Kanner,
Having left Germany
for the star-spangled banner.
In 1943, he published his paper,
On eleven boys and girls
and their autistic behaviour.
He borrowed the term from another physician.
But he was the first to call it a 'condition'.

But that's not all that Leo did –

He said the kids' challenges,
emotional and others,
Were all because
of their refrigerator mothers
Were all because
of their refrigerator mothers.
Were all because
of their refrigerator mothers.

Meanwhile, across the Atlantic Ocean,
Amidst the World War Two commotion.
Hans Asperger wrote a similar thesis
Was it coincidence or telekinesis?

Kanner's work was widely lauded
Asperger's, somewhat less applauded.
Until around nineteen hundred and eighty
When it received notoriety, baby
It even earned a place in the DSM,
But then DSM-5 kicked it out again.
It even earned a place in the DSM,
DSM-5 kicked it out again
DSM
DSM?
Diagnostic and Statistical Manual of Mental Disorders…

Off the back of Kanner's work
The medical industry went berserk
Treating and curing was all the rage
Let's wipe autism off the page.

We talk about treatments in the play.
But in the meantime, it's suffice to say
It came as a relief all round
When neurodiversity got off the ground.

When neurodiversity got off the ground.

This is where we're at today,
With a growing community.
It's not caused by vaccines or an epidemic,
In fact it's mostly genetic.
But that's all we
Can fit
into this song.
The rest is in a book called *Neurotribes*
by Steve Silberman.

11. Positive and Negative Reinforcement

A DOCTOR *delivers a lecture. Creepy horror music plays underneath the scene. Everything is heightened, not believable.*

DOCTOR. It's relatively simple. If the child achieves the desirable behaviour, we reward them with a biscuit.

ASSISTANT. And if that doesn't work?

DOCTOR. We look for another reward. Everyone loves something. The trick is to find what that thing is and use it.

ASSISTANT. And if they don't respond to rewards?

DOCTOR. Other measures can be introduced.

He demonstrates with an electric prodder.

ASSISTANT. You want to use that on children?

DOCTOR. Should we call them children, really? They're more primal in their instincts, more basic in their emotions and affections.

The ASSISTANT *struggles with this notion.*

Let's see it in action, shall we?

A CHILD *is brought in by* SECURITY GUARDS *and fitted with a system of wires.* DOCTOR *takes in the* ASSISTANT*'s expression.*

Don't look so worried. We'll start with something very light.

Screams.

ASSISTANT. Couldn't we try concentrating on the positives?

DOCTOR. We could. However, take Lewis, for example. No amount of positive reinforcement will stop the perpetual scratching he engages in.

ASSISTANT. But if we could teach him to do something else? A replacement behaviour.

DOCTOR *is sceptical.*

What about yesterday? He began to scratch, but I took his hand and showed him how to rub more softly. Wouldn't that be an option?

DOCTOR. Or we could increase the voltage?

ASSISTANT *is helpless as* DOCTOR *prepares to shock the* CHILD *again.*

INTERRUPTING VOICE. Hang on! That seems a little far-fetched.

VOICE. Not really.

INTERRUPTING VOICE. I know ABA isn't everyone's cup of tea, but...

VOICE. Listen to this: (*Produces a copy of the* Guardian *and reads.*) 'A video of electric-shock conditioning used inside the Judge Rotenberg Educational Center showed eighteen-year-old Andre McCollins being restrained face down, shouting for help from the people around him. His calls go unanswered, and he is given repeated shocks which cause him to scream in pain.'

The Judge Rotenberg Center (JRC) is a facility for children and adults with learning disabilities in Massachusetts.

INTERRUPTING VOICE. When was this? The seventies? Things have moved on.

VOICE. Really? In July 2018, there was an attempt by the State to try to get the centre closed down. But a family-court judge ruled that there was no evidence that JRC's methods are not an acceptable way of treating and caring for people with intellectual and developmental disabilities.

INTERRUPTING VOICE. Oh.

VOICE. I'll read on, shall I?

'McCollins, who spent six hours undergoing thirty-one shocks, was left in a catatonic state for a month afterwards.'

And then this: 'Students wear a backpack containing the shocking device, with electrodes constantly affixed to their skin. Staff are able to shock students at any point during the day.'

INTERRUPTING VOICE. In 2018.

VOICE. In 2018.

INTERRUPTING VOICE. So, this is still happening right now?

VOICE. Probably, yeah.

> INTERRUPTING VOICE *doesn't know what to say.*

12. Social Skills

FOUR. Loud noises coming up.

> *Chaos erupts. An exercise class.* KIDS*:* TERENCE, GINA *and* BEATRICE*, and their* PARENTS*. A sports instructor,* SIMON.

SIMON. Okay, guys. We're going to play a game with the ball. I'll roll it to you, and you roll it back to me.

> SIMON *rolls the ball to one of the* KIDS*. Ad lib, as the ball is passed back and forth. The* PARENTS *occasionally redirect the* KIDS*' attention back to the teacher.*

PARENT ONE. How old is she?

PARENT TWO. She'll be five in June. How old is your fella?

PARENT ONE. He's five and a half. Where's she going in September?

PARENT TWO. She's doing an extra year in pre-school while we try to get her a place in a unit.

PARENT ONE. Did you go private for the diagnosis?

PARENT TWO. We had to in the end. I couldn't wait any longer.

PARENT ONE. We had to too. We tried to get him into Joseph's, but he's only borderline intellectual disability, so they won't take him.

SIMON. Sorry, could you keep it down a bit?

PARENT ONE (*to* TERENCE). Pay attention to Simon! (*Back to* PARENT 2.) I don't know what it would take for them to diagnose an intellectual disability. He didn't speak a word until he was four.

TERENCE *stares at his mother, fully aware of the fact she's talking about him. Meanwhile,* GINA *has wandered into danger and the teacher steps in to rescue her.*

SIMON. Can I get everyone to pay attention?

PARENTS ONE *and* TWO *attend to their* KIDS *for a moment, before losing concentration again.*

PARENT TWO. She has ADHD as well, you see. We had to get that diagnosis so she'll be seen by the clinic.

PARENT ONE. They wouldn't see us. We didn't want to medicate him.

PARENT TWO. I know. I didn't want to put her on medication, but we wouldn't have got the other supports otherwise.

PARENT ONE. Do you notice a difference?

PARENT TWO. She's sleeping better, anyway.

PARENT ONE. That's good.

PARENT TWO. The only thing is she gets a bit down in herself. She says it's like all the colour is gone out of the world.

PARENT ONE. They come out with the maddest things, don't they?

They watch their KIDS *for a moment. The* KIDS *watch back.*

I know they say they've no empathy, but I swear I see it sometimes. Another child will be crying and he'll go and help. Or he'll get a little spark in his eye. I just think then that there's someone in there, you know?

PARENT TWO. Are you getting the DCA?

TERENCE. DCA. Domiciliary Care Allowance.

PARENT ONE. I'm getting it for his older brother, but not for him yet. I can't face the thought of going through the whole thing again.

PARENT TWO. It's like you're condemning them, isn't it?

PARENT ONE. Whatever happened to focusing on the positive?

PARENT TWO. Lucky she's still in nappies or we'd never have got a yes.

PARENT ONE. *He's* a flight risk, so that might do it for us.

The KIDS *begin to run around the space, following an invisible circuit.*

TERENCE. In this moment, I can feel the ground moving. I can hear the sound of the lawnmower outside. I can feel the breath of the child beside me. I can smell the damp of the mats, the sweat of the trampoline and the faintest hue of the earth as the season changes once again. I focus on this. I try to escape the words and the feeling of what I am and am not. What I can and cannot do.

GINA. My body is here, but my mind is high, high up. Travelled out of me, through the little holes in the roof, got caught in a wire. Travelled along the wire, found a space in the roof and thought about stopping, but decided instead to join the crow on the rooftop as off he flew, above the playground, further. To the sea now and past the sea. Upwards through the troposphere, stratosphere, mesosphere, thermosphere, exosphere...

BEATRICE (*to audience*). Loud noise coming up.

KIDS. OUTER SPAAAAAACE.

BEATRICE. You can talk all you like, but you'll never catch me now.

SIMON *looks around. The* KIDS *are gone.*

SIMON. That's the end of the class, I guess. See you next week. Goodbye.

SIMON *gives the* PARENTS *a disapproving look. They are oblivious.*

13. I Couldn't Take It Any More

A TV interview set-up.

MOTHER. It reached the point where I couldn't take it any more.

MOTHER *becomes teary.*

INTERVIEWER. Take your time.

MOTHER *gathers herself. She's ready.*

Can you tell us what happened the day Casper died?

MOTHER. We got up as usual. I had a list of things to do, but we got a call from the school he attended to say that they had been flooded and wouldn't open that day. So, of course that didn't go down well with Casper.

INTERVIEWER. Can you explain for our viewers how this would have manifested?

MOTHER. So, it starts with the flapping and the whine. Then the tears come. That boy could cry on demand. Then the head banging. And when that didn't work, he'd lash out at me. I'd to take the sweeping brush to him that day.

INTERVIEWER. So, how did the morning progress?

MOTHER. We'd no milk in the house. Casper, of course, couldn't understand that the only way to fix that was to go to the shop and buy some. So, he's crying for milk, but at the same time he's crying because he hates going to the supermarket. It would set him off, you know?

INTERVIEWER. Could you tell us how old Casper was at this stage?

MOTHER. He was eight.

INTERVIEWER. And did he have any language?

MOTHER. Not really.

INTERVIEWER. Had he ever had language?

MOTHER (*sings a TV jingle several times… '1, 2, 3 dot i.e., just log on and save money'*). Things like that. He'd sing them randomly.

INTERVIEWER. But no meaningful language.

MOTHER. None at all.

INTERVIEWER. That must have been tough.

MOTHER. It was impossible. All the care you give, and you get nothing back.

INTERVIEWER. How did it make you feel?

MOTHER. Hopeless, depressed. Like there was never going to be light at the end of the tunnel.

INTERVIEWER. So, there was no milk…

MOTHER. That's right.

She stops. The INTERVIEWER *indicates she should continue.*

Sorry. I finally get him into the car. He's screaming because I've put the wrong shoes on him, or he doesn't want to wear shoes or something. I can't remember.

INTERVIEWER. And when you get to the supermarket?

MOTHER. I lock him in the car. For his own good. He hates shopping, the lights, the noise. It was for his own good. I'd have been in and out in ten minutes, and he had the iPad.

INTERVIEWER. And when you got back to the car, he was gone, is that right?

MOTHER. He'd climbed out through the window. I swear, he was like Houdini. He could find his way out of anything. They're clever like that.

INTERVIEWER. And where did you find him?

MOTHER. Well, I heard him before I saw him. He'd headed inside, but he was crying and someone, a passer-by had stopped him and thought he must be lost and he's jabbering at her, so she assumes he must need help and she brings him to security. All the while, he's trying to get into the supermarket because he knows that's where I'm gone. They were doing their best, but he bolted outside to get away from them and all of a sudden, he's run out in front of a car.

INTERVIEWER. I see.

MOTHER. And then everyone's screaming at me. Like I'm a bad mother. I was doing my best.

INTERVIEWER. Of course.

MOTHER. But it was impossible, you know? Just an impossible situation.

INTERVIEWER. Was Casper hurt?

MOTHER. Not a scratch on him. Sometimes, I wish he'd been taken there and then.

INTERVIEWER. So, what was it about that day that was different from any other day? Or was there something different?

MOTHER. Not so much different as I had reached my limit.

INTERVIEWER. You couldn't take it any more.

MOTHER. We'd had worse days, we'd had better days, but I couldn't bear it any more… I was a prisoner in my own home. The school had called to say they'd be closed again the following day. I couldn't stand the thought of it.

INTERVIEWER. So?

MOTHER. I went in that night. He was sleeping. For a change. And he was so calm. In that moment, I wanted to keep him like that forever. I took the pillow and I put it over his face. He didn't even wake. Didn't feel a thing.

INTERVIEWER. And then?

MOTHER. And then I called the Gards and told them what I'd done.

INTERVIEWER. How long ago was that?

MOTHER. Four years.

INTERVIEWER. So, Casper would have been twelve now?

MOTHER. That's right.

CASPER. My name is Casper. I am not here.

INTERVIEWER. And what were the repercussions?

MOTHER. We went to court. The judge was very sympathetic. He put it down to the failings of the state. A lack of support from family or spouse. Depression. The fact that I pleaded guilty from the outset obviously helped.

INTERVIEWER. So, did you serve any time?

MOTHER. I wasn't afraid to face the consequences of what I'd done.

CASPER. They let you away with murder.

INTERVIEWER. How have you coped?

MOTHER. I won't lie to you, it's been a long road to get even to where I am today. But what's been overwhelming is… the outpouring of support. People like me.

CASPER. People who'd kill their children.

INTERVIEWER. People who'd like to kill their children.

This was not in the script.

MOTHER. To put it bluntly, yes.

INTERVIEWER. So, the ultimate legal repercussions were?

MOTHER. I received a four-year prison sentence… suspended. And I paid a fine. A donation, actually.

CASPER. What's the price of a life?

INTERVIEWER. And you don't think that leniency paves the way for other parents, carers to take the same action you did?

MOTHER. It would have gotten worse and worse.

CASPER. My name is Casper. I am not here.

MOTHER. I'm not proud of what I did, but I can't take it back.

CASPER. My name is Casper. I am not here.

MOTHER. I'd have killed him or he'd have killed me, eventually. With all the support, I've realised that I can make a contribution.

CASPER. My name is Casper. I am not here.

MOTHER. I've founded a charity for parents who would have had this burden put upon them. To make their lives a little easier.

CASPER. My name is Casper. I am not here.

14. The Names

A roll call.

THREE. Kazuno Soeda

SIX. Not here.

THREE. Ashlyn Ellis

FIVE. Not here.

THREE. Jayden Webb

TWO. Not here.

THREE. Jordan Webb

ONE. Not here.

THREE. Sarah Dubois-Gilbeau

FOUR. Not here.

THREE. Robbie Ballenger

SIX. Not here.

THREE. Andrew Freund Jr

FIVE. Not here.

THREE. Ari Ase

TWO. Not here.

THREE. Mya Ase

ONE. Not here.

THREE. John Savage

FOUR. Not here.

THREE. Malachi Lawson

SIX. Not here.

THREE. Hector Pizarro

FIVE. Not here.

THREE. Cheng Ting-hin

TWO. Not here.

THREE. Aurelia Castillo

ONE. Not here.

THREE. Samvith

FOUR. Not here.

THREE. Susan Gibson

SIX. Not here.

THREE. Daniel Gibson

FIVE. Not here.

THREE. Shashank Reddy

TWO. Not here.

THREE. Adeep Reddy

ONE. Not here.

THREE. Christopher Bosselman

FOUR. Not here.

THREE. Tyler Talmage

SIX. Not here.

THREE. Aidan Talmage

FIVE. Not here.

THREE. Heaven Watkins

TWO. Not here.

THREE. Sumitra

ONE. Not here.

THREE. Chloe Hobbs

FOUR. Not here.

THREE. Jacob Edwards

SIX. Not here.

THREE. Emma Rose Bingaman

FIVE. Not here.

THREE. Mason Jordan

TWO. Not here.

THREE. Jalen Goldsborough

ONE. Not here.

THREE. Jonathan Schmoyer

FOUR. Not here.

THREE. Michael Guzman

SIX. Not here.

THREE. Sanaa Cunningham

FIVE. Not here.

THREE. Noah Campbell

TWO. Not here.

THREE. Kentae Williams

ONE. Not here.

THREE. Sabrina Ray

FOUR. Not here.

THREE. Brianna Gussert

SIX. Not here.

THREE. Omar Omran

FIVE. Not here.

THREE. These are just some of the children with disabilities who were killed by their parents or grandparents between 2017 and 2019. These are just some of their names.

CASPER. My name is Casper. I am not here.

15. Casper

CASPER. Casper. A life. Born. Newborn. Pain. The way they picked me up.

Unexpected, unpredictable, hauled up from sleep. Never knowing when it could happen, where the hands would be, clothes scratching noisily against skin. An organ. A sense organ.

But I liked being held. There would be a jolt. Shockwaves. Insides thumping. And then holding. Firm. Steady. Pressure. Constant. Until they put me down. Cold in the places where arms had wrapped around. So lonely for touch that I wished I had never known what it was to have had it.

In the beginning, they held me. Then less. Then seldom. Then holding became restraint. Holding me back. Holding me down. Holding me still.

Words came to me, but couldn't find a way out.

Words betrayed me. Words would come in. And in the beginning, people would wait. Their words echoing inside me. Sounds contorting. Snaking. They look. Waiting. I look back. I see features. I put them together to make a face. I realise they want something back from me.

Try to breed a satisfactory response. Lights in my eyes. They keep talking and my attempts at words are choked as I swallow theirs. Glugging back their words. Water-boarded. Finally, poised, I push to get something out, but it vomits a slur. Doesn't reach them. Waiting turns to anger. I can't look at anger. Seeking comfort, I cling to the only vocalisation I can find. 'Washing machines live longer with Calgon.' I wait for them to turn away.

I can feel the Earth spin.
I can feel the Earth spin.
I can feel the Earth spin.

Do you know what that's like? No rest. And all I can do is spin with it.

Birthdays.

Birthday one: Noise, shouting. Sounds that sound wrong, too many voices… danger. Something's on fire. All eyes on me. I Scream.

Birthday two: A present so terrifying, I keep trying to put it in the bin.

They take it out and I'm sent to my room for being ungrateful. I can't stand being alone. Hours later, I awake to the sickly smell of cake. A peace offering. Wanting to please, I choke it down in fistfuls.

Birthday three: I want to keep quiet, but it's too much. 'Happy birthday to you. Happy Birthday to you. Happy Birthday, dear – ' Before they can say my name. I blow out the candles, think maybe that will quench the singing too. Singing changes to shouting. My shouts. I'm alone in my room. Later, I sneak downstairs… gorge on what's left of the cake, only to throw it all up again.

Birthday four: By now I have the hang of it. Presents. Candles. Song.

Cake. I'm all set. This year, they'll be happy with me. I'm going to make them proud. But they've given up. No presents… no song… no candles… no cake.

Talks with doctors. Talking like I'm not there. Nothing is held back. 'I'm here. I can hear you.' But the words don't come and so I drown them out. Hands over ears. 'He does that all the time.' 'One, two, three dot i.e., just log on and save money.' 'He's at it again.'

The holding stopped.
The bus started to come.
The training.
Tasks for biscuits. Tasks for sweets. Tasks for cake.

I begin to feel ill at the smell of margarine and sugar.

I can't think when still. I can't concentrate. When my body moves, my brain goes in straight lines, but now I have to stay in my chair. When I have to stay in my chair, all I can do is stay in my chair. Stay in my chair. Stay in my chair. Stay in my chair. Stay in my chair.

Stay in my chair. Stay in my chair. Stay in my chair. Stay in my chair.

'Well done. You can stay in your chair now. Have another sweet and we'll move you to mainstream.'

Mainstream.

Instruction: 'Open your school bag, get out your maths book and turn to page twenty-eight.'

Stay in my... What? Page twenty-eight? What book? I'm so busy staying in my chair, I've missed the instruction.

Heads turning as my arms begin to flap.

'Is there a problem?'

I couldn't hear you. The words don't form.

'Open your school bag, get out your maths book...'

School bag, great! Open it. I can do that.

Wait! What book? What book?

Laughing now.

'He's so stupid.'

I pick up the school bag and leave the room.

Home.

'I had another call from Mr Finlay today. Mainstream is a big chance for you. You can make normal friends. Have a normal life.'

Sorry, Mum. Nothing comes out.

'Just try to listen to what the teacher is saying.'

I will. I will. I will I will I will.

I go to my room and hit my head off the wall.
Scratch my elbow until it bleeds.

My life is an exercise in failure.

16. Living in an Illiteral World

FIVE. Think twice.
  Keep your eyes peeled.
  No need to bite my head off.
  Hold your horses.
  Now we're sucking diesel.
  You didn't lick it off a stone.
  I was taken by surprise.
  I'm on the fence about it.
  Don't push your luck.
  We have a big group today, so we're going to split you all
  in half.
  Don't count your chickens before they hatch.
  Hang on a minute.
  Back in two shakes of a little lamb's tail.
  Have you no cop on?
  I've got my eye on you.
  I want to pick your brain…
  There's more than one way to skin a cat.
  I nearly died, laughing.

  FIVE *leaves*. FOUR *enters*.

FOUR. I'm going to kill her when she gets back.

17. Question Time

SIX. Does anyone have any questions about the play at the
  moment?

  *The timer is turned. The audience may or may not ask
  questions.*

18. Disclosure

ONE (*to audience*). Loud music coming up.

> SANDRA *and her now boyfriend,* COLM, *are in a nightclub. It is loud.* SANDRA *is uncomfortable.*

SANDRA. I'm autistic.

COLM. I know. I saw your prints on Instagram. I love them.

SANDRA. Not AR-tistic, AU-tistic.

COLM. No, you're not.

SANDRA. Would you like to ask my psychologist?

COLM. But like, sorry… you look totally normal.

SANDRA. And?

COLM. It's a spectrum, right? I guess everyone's a bit autistic, really.

SANDRA. No, they're not. You're autistic or you're not.

> *Beat.*

COLM. But there's a scale, isn't there? You're obviously on the low end of it or the high end… you know… mild.

SANDRA. You wouldn't say that if you saw me on a bad day.

> COLM *is baffled.*

COLM. Is this some elaborate excuse to break up with me?

SANDRA. What?

COLM. I've had some bad experiences. I went on a few dates with this girl. She told me she had terminal cancer, and she couldn't see me any more. A year later, I bump into her with her new boyfriend.

SANDRA. I'm not trying to break up with you.

COLM. You're not lying?

SANDRA. I don't lie. Not well, anyway.

COLM. Okay. Great.

SANDRA. But I can't meet you in cafés or bars or clubs any more. Or like, I can, but I need to be able to choose where we go.

COLM. Is it the train-station thing again?

SANDRA. Yes. The music, the way sound bounces off the walls, the way there's no getting away from the light, the smells.

COLM. You really don't like it.

SANDRA. No.

COLM. Okay.

SANDRA. Okay, okay?

COLM. I really like you.

SANDRA. Thanks.

COLM. That's the bit where you say, 'I really like you too.'

SANDRA. Oh. Okay.

COLM. Do you?

SANDRA. Yeah. Isn't it obvious?

COLM, *relieved. A moment. He tries to kiss her.* SANDRA *suddenly breaks it.*

I have to text my mother.

SANDRA *leaves.* COLM, *left alone, but happy.*

19. Some of Us Are Listening

SIX. Some of us are listening. Even when we seem not to be, we can hear everything you say. You won't stop talking, and I won't stop running, but I can hear you. I hear you when you talk like I'm not there.

I hear your tone to others and your tone to me, and I know that they are not the same.

Some of us are listening. We can hear the squeak of the floorboards, the satisfying scratch of the sofa fabric under our nails, the hiss of the kettle, the hum-thunk-thunk-whirr-bangbangbangbang of the washing machine, a plane over the house, a helicopter in the night, the sound of your breathing, the scrape of the toothpaste, the unbearable squawk of wet footwear on floorboards, the volume too loud on next-door's TV, the unpredictable hums and clicks, off-kilter, unexpected musical notes that fly from your mouth.

We can hear it all.

These sounds form our world.

INTERRUPTING VOICE. I'm sorry. Do you mind if I mention something?

VOICE (*tired of questions*). Go ahead.

INTERRUPTING VOICE. It's just that you said way back on page four: 'It started out as a joke, but actually led to the whole neurodiversity movement. We'll come back to that later.'

VOICE. Yeah.

INTERRUPTING VOICE. And… we're on page fifty-three already, and there are only seven scenes left, none of which, I notice, are called 'Neurodiversity Movement'. Sooooo…are we going to come back to it or not?

VOICE. Yeah.

INTERRUPTING VOICE. When?

VOICE. Now.

20. Autism Is...

THREE. If you google 'symptoms of autism' –

ONE. a rabbit hole many confused parents find themselves going down –

FOUR. you get something like this:

SIX. Abnormal Body Posturing or Facial Expressions

FIVE. Abnormal Tone of Voice

ONE. Avoidance of Eye Contact or Poor Eye Contact

FOUR. Behavioural Disturbances

TWO. Poor motor skills

SIX. Delay in Learning to Speak

FIVE. Inappropriate Social Interaction

ONE. Intense Focus on One Topic

TWO. Lack of Empathy

FOUR. Problems With Two-Way Conversation

THREE. Repeating Words or Phrases

TWO. Repetitive Movements

THREE. Repeating Words or Phrases

SIX. Self-Abusive Behaviours

THREE. Repeating Words or Phrases

FOUR. Sleep Disturbances

FIVE. Social Withdrawal

THREE. Repeating Words or Phrases

FOUR. This list is adapted from a website called: medicinenet.com and you'll find many others like it on other websites. But here's the thing:

FIVE. I've always been super-sociable.

ONE. I was speaking in sentences at fourteen months.

THREE. I have no difficulty with eye contact.

TWO. My son has always had exceptional motor skills.

SIX. My autistic daughter has more empathy than the rest of my kids put together.

FOUR. Hands down, the best 'two-way' conversations I've ever had, have been at bedtimes with my autistic son.

FIVE. And my daughter doesn't use words like I do, but once I started listening in the right way, I realised she'd been talking to me all along.

ONE. And here's the other thing... what's the deal with 'symptoms'? Like, there are *symptoms* of a cold, there are symptoms of the flu. But autism doesn't have clear symptoms.

THREE. That's because it's not a disease.

ONE. Exactly. And the problem with treating it like it is one, is that everybody starts wanting to cure it. During my lifetime, I have experienced Play Therapy, ABA Therapy, Social Skills classes, the candida diet, the gluten-free diet, the casein-free diet, the dairy-free diet, chelation... the list goes on. All in an attempt to rid me of my autism. And do you know what happened? I changed. I went from being a really happy autistic person to being a really fucking UN-happy autistic person.

THREE. Autistic people aren't sick.

TWO. They don't need fixing or curing.

SIX. They're just wired differently.

FOUR. Hence...

ONE. The Neurodiversity movement.

THREE. Neurodiversity has been defined by neurodiverse writer, Nick Walker, as: 'the diversity of human brains and minds – the infinite variation in neurocognitive functioning within our species.'

ONE. So, neurodiversity isn't *just* about autism.

SIX. ADHD, Tourette's, Dyslexia and Dyspraxia all come under the umbrella of the neurodiversity movement.

TWO. And what does it actually do?

THREE. It promotes the idea that there's not something wrong with us, we're just different.

ONE. And we're living in a world that's not always designed to accommodate our needs. That's what makes it hard.

FOUR. And that's the issue a lot of autistic people have with ABA.

ONE. (Even the so-called 'good' kind.)

FOUR. It's all about trying to modify someone's behaviour.

THREE. Make them more 'typical'.

ONE. Instead of making a few changes to accommodate their needs.

FOUR. Another problem is that we've always relied on medical people to define autism, when the real experts, the ones in a position to define it, are the people who are actually autistic.

Here are some of the responses we got when we asked autistic people to define autism.

FIVE. Definition. Autism is…

ONE. Autism is the reason I currently have one thousand four hundred and twenty-three photographs of individual pancakes on my phone.

THREE. Autism is a trait, not a disease.

TWO. Autism is who I am.

SIX. Autism is a mental rewiring of the brain.

FOUR. Autism is an increase in universal volume and intensity.

FIVE. Autism is a natural part of evolution.

ONE. Autism has affected my life constantly, for better or for worse.

THREE. Autism is why I am fascinated by Home Video idents.

TWO. Autism is an awesome part of me that lets me be different.

SIX. Autism is a misunderstood thing.

21. The Science-y Bit

VOICE. And now, it's time for the science-y bit.

ONE. Loud music and singing coming up.

You've heard about the genome
Without it there'd be strife.

It's like a computer programme
That holds the code for life.

Each genome holds a complete set
Of an organism's DNA.
In humans, that's three billion pairs
Shaping life in every way.

Each cell holds this genome
Zoom in closer, look inside
The DNA's made of chromosomes
Where your genes reside

Many genes are passed straight down
From father and from mother.
Their combination makes you 'you'
And different from any other.

A lot of money has been spent
On finding autism's cause.
A lot of time's been wasted
'Cause the truth it always was…

That autism's genetic
It really is passed down.

Or caused by a mutation when
A new gene comes to town.

Autism's genetic
It really is passed down.
Or caused by a mutation when
A new gene comes to town.

They figured this out by studying twins
Identical and not.
They looked at all their findings
And this is what they got.

People who share most DNA
Are monozygotic twins,
And if one's autistic, there's an eighty-per-cent chance
That the other one also wins.

In testing dizygotic twins
The chances are much lower.
When one's autistic it's a fifty–fifty chance
The other will be a goer.

The fact that it's more likely shared
If twins are monozygotic
Meant the researchers finally proved
That autism's genetic.

Autism's genetic
It really is passed down.
Or caused by a mutation when
A new gene comes to town.

Autism's genetic
It really is passed down.
Or caused by a mutation when
A new gene comes to town.

And once the scientists found the proof
Of these genetic ties.
They could start to get much more precise
And find where autism lies.

But here's the thing: There are hundreds of genes
That so far fit the bill.
And while they might cause autism
There's no guarantee they will.

That's because the genome
We mentioned at the start.
While it's quite reliable,
Is not a precision art.

So, two identical embryos
That should be a carbon copy.
Depending how their programmes run.
Things can get a little sloppy.

If you go to a website called SFARI
There's a list of autism genes.
But meantime we can tell you
What this science really means...

ONE. Autism is genetic.

FIVE. You don't catch it; it's innate.

FOUR. But only in rare cases is it caused by a single genetic
mutation.

SIX. Autism is not caused by unemotional mothers.

TWO. Nor is it caused by vaccines, pollution, tuna fish, or any
other external factor.

THREE. Autism is a constellation of variations of the condition
known as life.

FIVE. And if a fraction of the money that's been spent on
autism research was spent on providing actual supports for
autistic people, then there'd be a lot more happy autistic
people in the world.

ALL (*sung*). There'd be a lot more happy
Autistic people in the world.

Autism's genetic
It really is passed down.

Or caused by a mutation when
A new gene comes to town.

Autism's genetic
It really is passed down.
Or caused by a mutation when
A new gene comes to town.

22. Questions Without Answers

PARENT. Why did you put your hands over your ears all the time?

CHILD. Why did it bother you when I did?

PARENT. Why could you not just do what you were told?

CHILD. Why did you keep asking me to do things I couldn't do?

PARENT. Why did it happen to us?

CHILD. Why was it such a disappointment?

PARENT. Why couldn't you be more like your brother?

CHILD. Why couldn't you take me as I am?

PARENT. Why didn't the therapy work?

CHILD. What made you think I was broken?

PARENT. Is it because I ate so much basil when I was pregnant?

CHILD. Why would you think that?

PARENT. Did it come from my side or your dad's side?

CHILD. Does that really matter?

PARENT. Did all the pollution in the city cause it? Or the pesticides in the food? Or the vaccinations?

CHILD. Why can't you stop looking at what you did wrong, and look at what you did right?

PARENT. Why can't someone invent a cure?

CHILD. Why would you cure someone who isn't sick?

PARENT. How are you going to live when I'm gone?

CHILD. How are *you* going to live when *I'm* gone?

23. Adult Diagnosis by the Public Health Service

A WOMAN *talks to an embodiment of the Public Health Service (PHS).*

PHS. NEXT!

WOMAN. Hi, I'm looking for an autism assessment.

PHS. For your child? You'll have to go to your GP for a referral. If the referral comes through, you'll have to wait eighteen months to three years to get into Early Intervention. If they age out of Early Intervention, you'll have to go on the School Age waiting list. That's about three years.

WOMAN. Not for my child. It's for myself.

PHS. No.

WOMAN. Sorry?

PHS. No.

WOMAN. No, I'm sorry. Maybe I'm not being clear. I'm looking to be assessed, to see whether I might have autism, be autistic, you know?

PHS. No.

PHS *waits for* WOMAN *to go away, but she doesn't.*

We don't do it.

WOMAN. Oh, right. Could you give me advice as to where I should go?

PHS. Go private.

WOMAN. But I can't afford to go –

PHS. NEXT!

WOMAN. Oh. Okay. Thanks, anyway.

24. Diagnosis in Later Life

During this text, WOMAN *is centre stage while the other actors perform 'circuits' of repeated choreographed movement around her.*

WOMAN. So, this is gas... there's a woman on the radio, right? And she says the first time she noticed her daughter was different, that she was autistic, was when she used to go around licking windows as a kid.

FIVE. And?

WOMAN. And it's ridiculous. I mean everyone licked windows, right?

FOUR. Eh...

WOMAN (*looking around for support*). Right?

No encouraging nodding.

(*To someone.*) Did you lick windows?

SIX. No.

WOMAN (*to someone else*). You?

FOUR. Nope.

WOMAN (*to another someone*). Did you?

FIVE. Eh... no-oh!

SIX (*to* WOMAN, *patronising*). Did *you* lick windows?

WOMAN. Yeah. Mirrors, too.

FOUR. Now that you mention it, I might have licked a mirror.

FIVE. I did it to practise kissing… does that count?

EVERYONE ELSE. No.

FOUR. Did you do it much? The window licking?

WOMAN. A good bit, I think.
    Enough to remember.
    To remember the feeling of different temperatures on
    my tongue.

    The different tastes.
    Different weathers.
    Raindrop-splattered versus damp, slightly mossy-flavoured
    glass.

TWO. Oh.

WOMAN. What?

TWO. Nothing.

WOMAN. What do you mean, 'Oh.'

TWO. Just, 'Oh.' It's interesting, that's all.

WOMAN. Why is it?

TWO. Why do you think?

    WOMAN *thinks*.

WOMAN. Oh. I see.

TWO. Yeah.

SIX. Anything else we should know?

WOMAN. When I was five, I was afraid of the rain.
    At the age of eight, I tried to become a Protestant.
    At the age of nine, I wanted to be a Communist.
    When I was eleven, I got nits and was so frightened of

Prioderm shampoo that I used to pick them out by hand to get rid of them. Nit by nit. Egg by egg.

FIVE. That's just gross.

WOMAN. I know.

At the age of fourteen, I stopped eating for the first time.
At the age of fifteen, I began to say 'scone' instead of 'scone'. 'Yogurt' instead of 'yogurt'.
At the age of seventeen, I could wrap these fingers around my upper arm and they would meet on the other side.
Until I was eighteen, the sound of a hoover made me cry.
I hate breaks.
Doing things I can't visualise terrifies me.
Sometimes, I don't realise people can see me.

The circuits stop.

FOUR. Well?

One person has said nothing up until now.

THREE. I think you passed.

WOMAN. Really?

THREE. I reckon so.

Welcome.

WOMAN. Thank you. Thank you so much.

WOMAN *finally gets to do a circuit. Everyone watches.*

THREE. I was twenty years old when I learned about my diagnosis.

TWO. I can't remember a time when I didn't know. It just took me longer to find my tribe.

ONE. I had to go through five different diagnoses before I finally landed at this one. It's like Cinderella and the glass slipper. You know when you've found the one that fits.

FIVE. I was thirty-nine years old when I received my diagnosis.

FOUR. I knew I was different, but not until my son's diagnosis did I realise why.

SIX. I will be seventy years old when I finally get my diagnosis and discover my community. It will be as if my life begins anew.

25. Happily Ever After

GORDON *is playing on his guitar. His* PARENTS *join him.*

MUM. Hi, Gordon.

GORDON *stops playing.*

GORDON. Hi Mum. Hi, Dad.

DAD. Hi, Gordon.

GORDON. Can you remember the morning I was born?

DAD. Your mum got up to get your brother and sister ready for school.

MUM (*to audience*). Gordon has two older siblings. Samantha is eight years older and Brian is four years older.

GORDON. Four years and four months.

MUM. Four years and four months.

DAD. I came down to get my lunch ready after the kids were off on the school bus. And your mum says to me, as calm as you like, 'I think I'm going to have the baby.'

MUM. You were already half out at this stage.

DAD. No time to get to the hospital.

MUM. You obviously weren't a fan of doctors, even then.

DAD. You were born right there in the middle of the kitchen.

MUM. And that's where you stayed for the next five years.

GORDON. In the house?

MUM. Right there. In the kitchen.

DAD. You couldn't stand any other room in the house.

MUM. We used to stick you in a wee drawer and your daddy would sleep there in the rocking chair and I'd come down for feeds.

GORDON. When did you know I was different?

MUM. From the very start. You were all different as far as I was concerned.

DAD. But there was something special about you.

GORDON. In what way?

MUM. It was like you'd been here before.

DAD. The health nurse even said it, when she came over to weigh you. It was like you'd seen it all before.

MUM. We used to call you The Judge.

DAD. It was like you were in here, in your little chair, watching us all and deciding on our fates.

MUM. As long as you were home, it made no difference to us. You were always a good boy. Maybe you didn't talk much, but with your brother and sister around it was hard to get a word in, anyway.

DAD. When you went off to school then, that's when it got hard for you.

GORDON. I couldn't cope.

MUM. The noise, so many other children. You'd have been delighted if they'd let you sit in a corner and read, but the teacher didn't think that was right.

GORDON. What did you think?

MUM. We just wanted to make things easier on you, you know? You had a very anxious few years. You'd be sick in the mornings before school. Crying on Sunday nights.

DAD. I suppose, with the diagnosis, we thought it might get you some support. You were such a good kid, and it was hard for you. You'd be getting into trouble and it wasn't your fault. You just couldn't cope.

GORDON. I remember.

GORDON *remembers*.

What was the worst thing about the diagnosis from your point of view?

MUM. I suppose, it was realising that some things – not all things, now, don't get me wrong – but that some things would be harder for you than they were for Brian and Samantha. And that that wasn't going to go away.

DAD. It was here to stay.

MUM. It's a part of you, isn't it?

GORDON. Yep.

DAD. And all we could do was support you. But we couldn't protect you for ever. Some things, we could help you with, and others, you'd have to do on your own.

MUM. And you did.

GORDON. And what was the best thing?

DAD. About the diagnosis?

GORDON. Yeah.

MUM. Waking up the next morning and realising nothing had changed. You were still you. We had a few answers now for why certain things were so hard. But nothing else had changed.

They are quiet.

GORDON. Thanks.

DAD. For what?

GORDON. For not trying to change me, or cure me, or whatever. Thanks for liking me the way I am.

26. The Last Bit

SIX. We're pretty much at the end of the play now. Can I ask you to do us a really big favour? At the end of the play, please don't clap.

THREE. Clapping makes me feel like my head is on fire.

TWO. Like the world is falling in on me.

ONE. If you feel like you want to do something, try giving us a flap instead.

They demonstrate.

FOUR. As we said at the start there's a talkback after the show, so if you'd like to stay and chat, please do.

FIVE. In your programme, you'll find a story, written for non-autistic people about how they can be more accommodating of autistic people. We hope you'll read it. If you're autistic and you think we've left out an important part of the story, please let us know.

TWO. All right, folks. That's the end of the performance. I hope you enjoyed it. Thank you very much.

The End.

A different kind of social story

There are more than 7.7 billion people in the world.

If all these people lined up side-by-side, each one would be different.

Each one would be unique.

Even identical twins... even their DNA isn't 100% the same.

Of the more than 7.7 billion people in the world, it is estimated that more than 1% of them are autistic.

That's over 77 million people in the world who are autistic.

This is a story about how people who are not autistic might begin to understand more and make more accommodations for the many citizens of the world, both children and adults, who are autistic.

Over the past number of years, there has been great progress worldwide in something called Autism Awareness. This is a wonderful step forward.

The next step is Understanding. Here are some things that non-autistic people might like to understand about autistic people:

Being autistic can mean that the brain develops differently to the typical brain. How the different parts of the autistic brain talk to each other and work together may be different too.

Autism is pervasive. Pervasive means that it affects basically everything about a person – their personality, memories, thoughts, how they grow up, how they communicate, how they think and move.

All autistic people are different to each other, but there are a few things most autistic people have in common, to varying degrees.

Information – Autistic people can process information atypically to their non-autistic peers. The way someone with autism looks at the world, perceives it, processes what they're experiencing, and then thinks about what they're experiencing is different to how non-autistic people experience the world around them.

Language – Autistic people have different abilities or capacities for language. Some autistic people don't naturally think in language, perhaps perceiving and thinking using visuals or abstract feelings instead. Using words, in spoken or written language, isn't first nature to many autistic people. Therefore, many autistic people spend a lot of time trying to translate the world around them.

Sensory – Autistic people have atypical sensory experiences. Some autistic people are oversensitive to sensory input, some are under-sensitive to sensory input, and some autistic people are both!

The information above may help non-autistic people to understand more about why autistic people may behave and communicate atypically.

Autistic children are often sent to social skills classes in order to learn about how to interact with non-autistic people in everyday situations.

Carol Gray introduced Social Stories in 1991 as a tool to help autistic people to prepare for everyday situations.

But here's the thing… recent research showed that typical brains are already programmed to identify and reject difference, so autistic people can learn all the social skills they're *expected* to have, but they may still struggle to be accepted.

So, that leads to the third step: Autism Acceptance. And that's why this story has been written.

It's likely that non-autistic people regularly meet people with autism, even if they don't always realise it.

When meeting someone who is autistic, a non-autistic person can try to remember these things:

Presume intelligence and competence. Even if someone doesn't speak or communicate in a typical way, they may still have a lot of interesting and valid things to say.

Anxiety is a big part of autism. Non-autistic people can try to be gentle and kind, without being patronising. Using a softer tone of voice can be a big help here.

Autistic people often have sensory differences that mean they can be sensitive to particular noises, lights, textures, touch and more. Even if these sensitivities aren't shared by non-autistic people, it will usually help autistic people if their sensitivities are accepted as valid, and accommodated rather than being dismissed.

Autistic people can sometimes take longer to process information. When asking a question, a non-autistic person can wait eight seconds for an answer. If they don't receive an answer, they can then repeat the question, using the same words in the same order. It may help to say the autistic person's name before asking them a question.

Some autistic people enjoy hugs. Some don't. A non-autistic person can check if the autistic person would like a hug before hugging them.

Autistic people don't need to be changed or fixed. Just because someone is different doesn't make them less.

These are some things that might help to build a world where autistic people are fully accepted.

But here is something very important: just like each of the 7.7 billion people on this planet is unique, each autistic person is also unique.

In the words of Dr Stephen Shore: 'If you've met one person with autism, you've met one person with autism.'

Each autistic person is different and has different needs.

When a non-autistic person meets an autistic person, they can try not to make any assumptions about that person or their unique needs.

They can try to listen and be curious instead. Listening, curiosity and taking time may enable an autistic person to share more about themselves.

There are over 7.7 billion people on the planet.

Each one is different.

Each one is unique.

Together, autistic and non-autistic people can work to build a world where each one of those citizens is accepted.

Jody O'Neill and Eleanor Walsh

Sources

Employment Statistic
National Autistic Society – https://www.autism.org.uk/get-involved/campaign/employment.aspx

Isolation Rooms
Inclusion Ireland – http://www.inclusionireland.ie/content/media/1701/department-education-inaction-unregulated-seclusion-and-restraint-practices

MMS
https://www.rte.ie/news/2018/0215/941028-bleach

https://www.thejournal.ie/hse-bleach-staff-autism-3708653-Nov2017

https://www.irishtimes.com/news/health/doctor-at-centre-of-prime-time-report-is-struck-off-1.2803505

https://www.independent.ie/irish-news/it-is-pure-child-abuse-irish-dad-accused-of-feeding-son-6-bleach-to-cure-his-autism-36080430.html

Judge Rotenberg Center
https://www.theguardian.com/education/2018/jul/12/judge-rotenberg-educational-center-electric-shocks

The Names
https://disability-memorial.org/

Symptoms of Autism
https://www.medicinenet.com/autism_symptoms_and_signs/symptoms.htm

Neurodiversity Definition
https://neurocosmopolitanism.com/neurodiversity-some-basic-terms-definitions

www.nickhernbooks.co.uk

facebook.com/nickhernbooks

twitter.com/nickhernbooks